THOMAS BECKET

English Saint and Martyr

LEADERS OF THE MIDDLE AGES™

THOMAS BECKET — English Saint and Martyr

David Hilliam

BPMS MEDIA CENTER

The Rosen Publishing Group, Inc., New York

Published in 2005 by The Rosen Publishing Group, Inc.
29 East 21st Street, New York, NY 10010

First Edition

Library of Congress Cataloging-in-Publication Data

Hilliam, David.
Thomas Becket: English saint and martyr / David Hilliam.— 1st ed.
    p. cm. — Leaders of the Middle Ages
Includes bibliographical references and index.
ISBN 1-4042-0165-3 (library binding)
1. Thomas Becket, Saint, 1118?–1170. 2. Great Britain—History—
Henry II, 1154–1189—Biography. 3. Christian martyrs—England—
Biography. 4. Christian saints—England—Biography. 5. Statesmen—Great
Britain—Biography.
I. Title. II. Series.
DA209.T4H55 2005
942.03'1'092—dc22
                                                          2004004547

Manufactured in the United States of America

On the cover: Background: A thirteenth-century illuminated manuscript page showing the assassination of Thomas Becket. Inset: Image of Saint Thomas Becket, archbishop of Canterbury. A detail from circa 1280 window at Canterbury Cathedral.

CONTENTS

LAND AT THE TIME OF THOMAS BECKET

INTRODUCTION: A CLASH BETWEEN A KING AND AN ARCHBISHOP

The history of Thomas Becket, archbishop of Canterbury, is a powerful drama set in twelfth-century England. It is the story of an immense struggle for power between church and state. The two men representing each side of this struggle were King Henry II of England and Thomas Becket. Henry II ruled from 1154 to 1189, and Thomas Becket was the archbishop of Canterbury from 1162 to 1170.

It is important to realize that these men lived a century before any form of parliament had been developed in England or anywhere else in medieval Europe. Kings such as William the Conqueror, of England, or Philip Augustus, of France, were all-powerful

in the countries where they ruled. In England, there was a Great Council. This consisted of the most important noblemen in the land. However, the council met only on rare occasions, when the king wanted it to meet. Even then, the king decided what the council could discuss.

English kings were dictators. It was not until the next century—during the reign of King John (1199–1216)—that some limits were put on their powers. This occurred in 1215, when the English barons (noblemen and landholders) forced King John to sign the important set of rights defined in the famous document known as the Magna Carta.

In the twelfth century, however, Henry II had nearly unlimited authority throughout his extensive landholdings in England and France. The one exception was the Roman Catholic Church—and this was of extreme importance. All clergy owed loyalty to the king. However, they also owed loyalty to the head of the church in England: the archbishop of

This is Thomas Becket, as depicted in a stained-glass window in Canterbury Cathedral. Shortly after Becket's death, Canterbury Cathedral was extensively enlarged and new stained-glass windows were installed. The artist who made this famous window might well have seen Becket during the time he was archbishop.

Canterbury. The archbishop owed loyalty to the king, but also to the pope in Rome. The pope was the supreme head of the church. He was believed to be God's representative on Earth. As such, he was viewed as God's spokesperson.

For most of the time, this arrangement presented no difficulty. Church matters were usually separate from affairs of state. This way, kings and archbishops were able to maintain their different areas of influence. There had to be discussion between the kings and archbishops whenever new appointments had to be made. However, there were usually no grounds for serious disagreement.

When Henry II came to the throne in 1154, England had just emerged from a period of civil war. Henry was determined to bring law and order to the country. He was passionate about getting rid of the bad practices and customs that had developed during the previous reign.

Only twenty-one years of age, Henry had energy and determination. He constantly traveled through his kingdom to look for anything that was wrong either among his nobles or his churchmen. His nobles were often becoming too powerful, living in castles that he had not allowed them to build. Also, priests and other churchmen were literally getting away with murder. Henry was angry to find that clergy members who committed offenses were not brought before ordinary courts of law. Instead, they were dealt with by their fellow clergymen, who often gave light punishments or even let them off altogether. Obviously, this matter needed to be investigated. Henry felt that everyone, including the clergy, should be subject to the king's laws and not treated separately.

In the process of trying to tidy up the laws of the land, Henry was beginning to interfere with the traditional rights of the church. There were other matters, too, in which he found himself disagreeing with the bishops. However, it was not until Thomas Becket was appointed archbishop of Canterbury that the rivalry for power developed into a long and bitter dispute.

Thomas Becket believed that the church was far more important than the state. To him, it was clear that God's affairs were greater than those of the king. Therefore, he felt that the king had no business interfering with church matters. As archbishop of Canterbury, he had God-given authority to resist King Henry whenever he thought that the king was interfering with the church and its clergy.

On his part, King Henry had no doubt that all members of the church should obey him and the

This is an image of the Miracle Windows in Canterbury Cathedral. Shortly after Becket's death, two monks, William and Benedict, collected accounts of all the miracles said to have occurred at his tomb. In 1200, stained-glass artists illustrated these stories and filled the windows around Becket's shrine with beautiful pictures.

laws of England. He felt that this was especially true if they had committed crimes. Henry believed that no person should be above the law—even the archbishop of Canterbury.

Clearly, these two points of view were in opposition. Both Henry and Thomas were men of extraordinary strength of character. The clash of personalities and resulting arguments had consequences that were felt for many centuries—long after both men had died.

KING HENRY II— THE HISTORICAL BACKGROUND

King Henry II ruled England during Thomas Becket's lifetime. Born in 1133, Henry was the son of Geoffrey Plantagenet, Count of Anjou. Anjou was a large province in France. Henry's mother, Matilda, was a granddaughter of William the Conqueror's. William was a Norman duke who had invaded England in 1066 and had become its king after defeating the Saxon army (led by King Harold) in the Battle of Hastings. Matilda played an important role in the history of England. At one time, she had been England's ruler. In that role, she was given the special title of Lady of the English.

It is important to know the circumstances that led to Matilda's receiving this unusual title. Her father, King Henry I, had been the youngest and smartest son of William the Conqueror's. Henry I was a wise and strong ruler. He was also determined to bring peace and order to the kingdom that had been recently conquered by his father. There were still areas that were strongly opposed to the Norman invaders. He reigned for thirty-five years (1100–1135). His nicknames were Beauclerc, meaning that he was well educated, and Lion of Justice, which suggests a love of law and order.

The great tragedy of Henry's life became known as the "white ship disaster." His two sons, William and Richard, were both drowned in a brand-new boat that was sailing on its first voyage off the coast of Normandy. As a result, Henry was filled with grief and disappointment. Apart from his personal loss, the drowning accident meant that England had no male heir to succeed to the throne. Henry's first wife died and he married again, but there were no children from this second marriage. The result was that as he neared the end of his life, he decided to make his daughter Matilda his heir.

HENRY II'S MOTHER: THE EMPRESS MATILDA

Although it was extremely unusual to give the power of a monarchy to a young woman, Matilda was no

THE HOLY ROMAN EMPIRE

The title of Holy Roman Emperor was given to the successors of Charlemagne. Charlemagne was a great ruler in the ninth century, and his vast empire consisted of most of Europe. When he died in 814, the empire was quickly broken up. However, the title of Holy Roman Emperor remained. Various German kings held the title until it was abandoned in 1806. Just as the pope was the leader of the Roman Catholic Church throughout Europe, the Holy Roman Emperor was considered to be the leader of all the kings and rulers. In practice, however, it was merely a title with no power attached to it.

In this illustration from Les Grandes Chroniques de France (The Great Chronicles of France), *the first Holy Roman Emperor, Charlemagne (747–814), is seen with his ambassadors. This is a some-what fanciful picture, made in the fifteenth century. Charlemagne's great empire remained in people's imagination for centuries after it had been broken up.*

ordinary woman. She was the daughter and grand-daughter of kings. As such, her position commanded respect. In 1114, when she was only twelve years old, she was married to the Holy Roman Emperor. She learned German and went to live in Germany. Because of this marriage, she is often referred to as the Empress Matilda. Her husband, the emperor, died in 1125. She later married Geoffrey IV (the Handsome), the Count of Anjou. They had three sons, the most important of whom was to become Henry II of England.

However, the story of Matilda as ruler of England is one of bitter dispute. Just before his death in 1135, her father, Henry I, had called his nobles together and made them all swear an oath of loyalty and obedience to Matilda as their future queen once he had died. At that time, the idea of having a ruling queen was not acceptable. It was unthinkable to put a woman on the throne during this period of history. It was a male-dominated world. Nevertheless, they all swore to give Matilda their support, including Henry's nephew Stephen, who was thirty-eight years of age.

Matilda must have been outraged when, after her father died, Stephen seized the throne. To make matters worse, he was supported by many of the

This is an image of King Stephen, who was king of England from 1135 to 1154. In fact, he was a usurper, seizing the throne of England from the rightful queen, Matilda. The whole of his reign was marked by civil strife as Matilda struggled to become England's ruler. Matilda was the mother of King Henry II of England. This illuminated manuscript dates from the early fourteenth century and comes from the *Anglo-Norman Chronicle* by Peter Langtoft.

nobles who had previously sworn their loyalty to Matilda. Immediately, she gathered her own supporters and attacked Stephen's armies.

The history of Stephen's reign is a confused tangle. During this civil war, there were battles, imprisonments, and supporters who kept switching sides. At one time, Matilda's forces actually managed to capture Stephen. However, he was

PLANTAGENET DYNASTY

The name "Plantagenet" has an interesting history. It comes from Count Geoffrey of Anjou's (Henry's father) habit of wearing a sprig of yellow broom flower on his helmet as an identifying emblem. The scientific name for broom is *Planta genista*.

Thirteen more kings of the Plantagenet dynasty ruled England from 1154 to 1485. The Plantagenet dynasty was by far the longest in English royal history.

This is a medieval illustration showing Geoffrey of Anjou, the second husband of Matilda.

released in exchange for her illegitimate half brother, Robert. Matilda herself was captured twice but managed to escape both times. On one occasion, she disguised herself as a corpse, dressed in a shroud. Another time, she lowered herself down by rope from the top of a castle tower in Oxford (the tower still stands).

The civil war lasted for nearly twenty years. Finally, Stephen and Matilda came to an agreement. Stephen would remain king for the rest of his life, and then, after his death, the throne would pass to Matilda's son, Henry. However, Stephen died unexpectedly of appendicitis quite soon after this arrangement had been made. Then, Matilda's son, Henry, was welcomed into England. He was a strong and determined young man who restored law and order to a country that had suffered immensely during the weak reign of King Stephen.

THE CHARACTER OF KING HENRY II

Matilda's son, Henry Plantagenet, began his reign in 1154 when he was twenty-one years old. The members of the Plantagenet dynasty (family of rulers) would continue to rule England for the next 341 years. They finally gave way to the Tudors (the family of rulers that succeeded the Plantagenets) after losing the Battle of Bosworth in 1485.

Henry was the most powerful monarch in Europe. Not only did he possess England, but he was also Duke of Normandy and Count of Anjou. He had also recently married the richest woman in the known world—Eleanor of Aquitaine. Eleanor owned Aquitaine, an immensely valuable province in the south of France. In addition, she owned two other rich provinces: Poitou and Guienne. As a result of marrying Eleanor, Henry could boast of being in control of more territory than anyone else in Europe. It was a vast empire, and he needed all his determination and energy to rule over it.

England had never been ruled by such a dynamic and forceful king. Henry was constantly on the move, throughout England and his lands in France. In fact, he ordered all the abbeys in England to keep horses ready for him in case he happened to arrive suddenly and was in need of them. His abilities when waging war against his enemies were terrifying. He was passionately interested in law and enjoyed attending his courts of law.

In terms of his personality, he was mostly friendly and approachable. However, whenever anyone crossed his will, he had a terrible and uncontrollable temper. Because he was constantly active, he usually ate his meals standing up. No one ever knew until the last moment what he would do

This is an illuminated manuscript page showing Thomas Becket, archbishop of Canterbury, and Henry II. The two men are arguing. This illuminated manuscript page, which comes from the *Anglo-Norman Chronicle*, dates from the first quarter of the fourteenth century. The work was written in French in rhyming verse by Peter Langtoft, who died circa 1307.

or where he would go next. Life for Henry's servants and advisers was hectic and unpredictable.

Henry's wife and queen was a powerful woman in her own right. Also, according to everything her contemporaries wrote about her, she was extremely beautiful. She had become Duchess of Aquitaine when she was only fourteen. Then, a year later, she had married Louis, the heir to the French throne. Almost immediately afterward, the king of France died.

After his death, Louis and Eleanor became king and queen of France. Her marriage to King Louis lasted fifteen years. During that time, she took part in the Second Crusade. She actually led a party of noblewomen on what was called a Ladies Crusade. However, she thought that Louis was dull. Eventually, she asked for a divorce. Only a few months later, she married Henry, Count of Anjou. This is what he was called before he became king of England. They were obviously deeply attracted to one another despite their twelve-year age difference.

Henry's reign was a long and busy one. He was constantly fighting enemies who were trying to seize his lands in France. Overall, he enjoyed peace and tranquillity in England. However, he had trouble with the Scots, Welsh, and Irish, who were always fighting for their independence. Henry's main worries in England came from his conflict with the church, which was led by Thomas Becket. It was a conflict that lasted for eight years, from 1162 to 1170. In hindsight, the conflict between Henry and Thomas Becket was as important as any of the military battles Henry ever fought.

THOMAS BECKET'S EARLY LIFE

CHAPTER 2

Thomas Becket was born in London in 1118. This time was still within living memory of the Battle of Hastings. At that battle, the Norman ruler, William the Conqueror, had killed King Harold and made himself king of England.

The London in which Thomas Becket grew up was much smaller than the London of today. It was a walled city with a population of only about 16,000. It had eight large gates that could be closed against enemies.

Thomas's father was a prosperous merchant who lived in Cheapside, which was at that time the principal shopping street in London. Both his parents had come from Normandy in France. This was an important advantage to Thomas as he grew up. After the Norman invasion, those who could speak Norman French and had a French background were much more at ease with the Norman lords who had become the rulers.

Fortunately for Thomas, one of his father's friends, a wealthy Norman baron called Richer de Laigle, took a liking to him. The baron frequently invited Thomas to his castle at Pevensey on the south coast of France. He taught Thomas how to ride like a knight and how to joust and go hawking. These were both very popular sports among the Norman nobles. The baron also taught Thomas how to behave properly in high society. These lessons were going to be important for Thomas in his later life, when he would be associating with kings and noblemen.

Like many boys, Thomas was sent away to a monastery at age ten to be educated by monks. At first, he went to Merton Priory, near London. Then, when he was older, he went to another school in London itself. From there, he went to study for a few years in Paris. He learned Latin, divinity (religious studies), and rhetoric (how to express oneself properly and make speeches). These were the usual subjects taught in those days. It was probably as good an education as most young men could get. This was because, at that time, there were hardly any universities in Europe.

THE DEVELOPMENT OF UNIVERSITIES

Universities were just beginning to be established during the lifetime of Thomas Becket. The University of Bologna, in Italy, which was founded in 1088, was famous for its law studies. The University of Paris was founded circa 1150, and the Universities of Oxford and Cambridge began in the twelfth century. Around 1145, Becket was fortunate enough to be sent to Bologna, which at the time was the only school that specialized in law.

In this illuminated manuscript page, Philip Augustus, king of France from 1180 to 1223 (shown here on the left), grants the first royal privilege to graduates and students at the University of Paris. The University of Paris was one of the earliest universities in Europe. It was founded circa 1150.

After about three years of working as a secretary, Becket came across some good fortune when he was twenty-five. He was recommended as a promising young man to serve in the household of a very important man, Theobald, archbishop of Canterbury. Here, he quickly became noticed as a dependable, hardworking member of the archbishop's staff. In particular, he seemed to have a special gift for diplomacy. He was sent on missions to Rome and went with Theobald to many extremely important conferences. There, he met churchmen from many countries. Also during this period, Theobald sent Becket to study law at Bologna in Italy and then at Auxerre in France. It was clear that Becket was being encouraged to make a very good career for himself.

BECKET AS THE ARCHBISHOP'S REPRESENTATIVE

Perhaps the most important task entrusted to Becket was to act on Theobald's behalf when King Stephen of England wished to have his son, Eustace, crowned. Crowning the heir to the throne during the lifetime of his father was a curious practice. It was intended to ensure a smooth succession in the event of the death of the older king.

However, Stephen was not popular and Archbishop Theobald was not in favor of crowning Eustace. Because of the civil war in England, the archbishop did not think it was wise to leave the country. Therefore, he sent Thomas Becket to Rome in his place. Becket was to persuade the pope to disagree to the proposed coronation. Stephen, of course, tried to get his way. However, Becket was successful in arguing Theobald's case, and the idea was dropped.

Although he was still a young man, Becket was quickly making influential friends. As a result, the archbishop gave Becket many valuable "livings," meaning posts within the church. In modern times, it would be considered a scandal to hold several jobs within the church at the same time. However, during the Middle Ages, it was common for clergy to accept financial rewards for work that they did not actually perform. The bishop of Worcester gave Becket the living of the church of Mary-le-Strand in London. Archbishop Theobald gave him the living of Otford in Kent. As well, he was given a "prebend" (a share in the revenues) at St. Paul's Cathedral in London and another prebend at Lincoln Cathedral in Lincolnshire.

The most valuable appointment came to him in 1154 at the age of thirty-six. He became archdeacon of

This is Archbishop Theobald's seal. It shows him standing robed for Mass, holding his archbishop's pastoral staff in his left hand. The staff, which is shaped as a shepherd's crook, is called a crozier. He is raising his right hand in blessing. Traditionally, a bishop or archbishop carries a crozier to remind his people that he, like Christ, is a Good Shepherd.

Canterbury—one of the highest church posts in England. An archdeacon is the chief supervisor of a diocese—in this case, the important diocese of Canterbury. An archdeacon ranks just below the bishop of a cathedral. In Canterbury, Becket came next in rank to the archbishop himself.

Becket cannot be criticized for holding all these posts at the same time. It is simply the way things were done. In medieval times, a successful man gained wealth and distinction by being linked in this way to the all-powerful church.

Curiously, at the time Becket became archdeacon of Canterbury, he was not even a priest. He became ordained as a deacon when he took on the post of archdeacon. Even this ordination was not the equivalent of being a priest, which included the special power of pardoning sins. At this period of his life, Becket did not appear to have ambitions to hold high rank in the church. While he did attend Mass and believe in the church's teachings, the priesthood was not foremost in his mind. Early in his career, Becket had been involved in the dispute between the supporters of Matilda and those of Stephen, as each of them claimed the throne.

BECKET AND KING HENRY II

In the same year that Becket became archdeacon of Canterbury, King Stephen died. Henry Plantagenet, Duke of Anjou, became king of England. It is probable, but not known for certain by historians, that Becket played a part in this. More specifically, it is thought that Becket took part in the political negotiations that led to Henry becoming king. Earlier in his career, Becket had been involved in the dispute over crowning King Stephen's son.

With the new king, there was a different atmosphere in England. Stephen's rule had been disastrous. Everyone looked to Henry to restore peace after the long civil war. Obviously, Henry needed competent administrators to carry out his plans. One of his top priorities was to find a new chancellor to be his chief executive and personal assistant. He asked Archbishop Theobald's advice on whom to choose.

Theobald was somewhat suspicious of the new king, who was young, ruthless, and headstrong. In fact, Theobald suspected that Henry might impose new laws that would limit the freedom of the clergy and, furthermore, that these would be against the interests of the church. Accordingly, he decided to recommend his own trusted servant, Thomas Becket, to be the king's chancellor. He believed that Becket would help to protect the church if any disputes arose.

Many influential people supported the choice of Becket as chancellor, including Henry of Blois, bishop of Winchester and brother of the late King Stephen. On these recommendations, King Henry felt safe in making the appointment. In 1155, Becket became the king's chancellor and the second-most important person in the kingdom. It is clear that Thomas Becket had impressed everyone he met with his abilities as an administrator.

THE POST OF KING'S CHANCELLOR

Most modern countries, such as the United States, Canada, and Great Britain, have developed a democratic form of government. These democracies often consist of an upper and lower body of statesmen and politicians.

At present, England has its House of Commons and House of Lords, which together make up the Houses of Parliament. It is difficult to imagine a time when countries were ruled by a king who was helped and guided by a relatively small number of advisers.

However, in the time of Henry II, kings had absolute power. As such, no king could possibly carry out all the affairs of state by himself. There had to be someone who would attend to the king's wishes and make sure that everything ran

This is a photo of Thomas Becket's personal seal, made of an antique gem probably acquired in Paris or Bologna. It shows a figure, which may be a representation of Mercury, Mars, or Perseus. The letters in the center spell out "Seal of Thomas of London." In addition, Becket would have had official seals as archdeacon or archbishop.

smoothly. This was the enormous responsibility of the chancellor.

Acting as the king's secretary, the chancellor accompanied the king everywhere. He attended all meetings, large or small, and dealt with every important administrative document. He was also solely in charge of the king's Great Seal of England. This metal seal was used to give authority to important state documents and prove that the king genuinely approved them. The seal, which had an impression of the king on both sides, was pressed onto heated wax. This was then pressed down onto any document that required it, thus adhering the wax seal to the document.

The chancellor was closely involved in all matters of state finance. For example, he kept records of the country's expenses. He also acted as the king's chaplain and was very influential in appointing bishops and other high-ranking churchmen. In short, there was virtually nothing of importance in the entire country that did not involve the chancellor. Naturally, Becket had a huge salary for doing all this.

Unmarried and in his mid-thirties, Thomas Becket was just about to enjoy the marvelous lifestyle that came with the chancellorship.

Becket: The King's Chancellor

From the beginning of his time as chancellor, Becket delighted in showing off his power and wealth. It is probable that no one in England before him had given such wonderful banquets to so many people.

His hospitality became legendary. He entertained with extraordinary foods and superb wines. Anyone who needed to see him or the king was welcomed to his feasts. However, his extravagant lifestyle was not limited merely to eating and drinking. Becket also had a passion for magnificent clothes and fine horses. In addition, he had a large number of servants at his disposal. Along with that, he had the use of a fleet of six superbly equipped ships. These would transport him—and all his attendants—to and from France whenever he wanted to travel.

Becket continued to work hard, and Henry trusted him completely. In fact, he treated him as his closest friend. It was clear that the two men were on the best of terms. The king would frequently go to Becket's house simply for the pleasure of his company. He would drop in casually after hunting and enjoy whatever was being served at the dining table. Henry himself did not appear to be jealous of Becket's extravagant way of living. Perhaps this lifestyle amused him. He himself hardly ever relaxed or indulged in luxuries. However, if his chancellor chose to enjoy the good things in life, Henry would not be critical of his extravagance so long as Becket worked hard and was loyal on his behalf.

Together, king and chancellor brought firm rule to the country. Henry insisted on total obedience from everyone. He quickly got rid of many abuses. In particular, he forced the barons who had become too powerful during Stephen's reign to tear down their castles if they were not properly approved of by the king. Only the king could allow fortifications to be built. Barons were required to seek the king's permission before being granted a "license to crenellate"—meaning, build a fortified castle. Henry and Becket enjoyed the challenge of governing England with justice.

BECKET AND THE PROPOSED ROYAL MARRIAGE

At the time, relations between King Henry and King Louis of France were not good. Louis was aware that when his former wife, Eleanor of Aquitaine, had divorced him, she had married Henry within months. It was widely known, too, that she had complained that life with Louis was like being married to a monk. Louis was also envious that Henry controlled a larger area of France than he did himself. As for Henry, although he possessed most of France, there was an area owned by Louis that Henry also wanted. Called the Vexin, it lay on the western border of Henry's own province of Normandy.

In 1158, Henry came up with a proposal that he hoped would not only heal the rift between the two countries but also give him the Vexin. His idea was to arrange a marriage between his own son, also named Henry, and Louis's daughter, Margaret, a child from his second marriage. The proposal included the request that the Vexin be given to him as part of the French princess's dowry.

The main problem with this marriage arrangement was that the couple involved in it were far too young. Henry, the proposed bridegroom was only three, and Margaret was just a few months old! Nevertheless, the

THE CUSTOM OF GIVING A DOWRY

A dowry is a gift that the family of the bride is expected to give to the family of the bridegroom. In most Western countries, the custom of giving a dowry at a marriage has almost been completely forgotten. However, it still exists in some parts of the world, such as India. In the Middle Ages, the dowry of a royal bride was extremely valuable—it could even be whole towns or tracts of land. Henry received a generous dowry from Louis on the proposed marriage of his son to Louis's daughter.

This image shows Louis VII, king of France from 1137 to 1180, and Eleanor of Aquitaine, who was his wife at the time. This French illuminated manuscript (dating from circa 1335 to 1340) shows the two as they are getting a divorce. This image is from Les Grandes Chroniques de France. *Their divorce took place in March 1152, and shortly afterward, Eleanor married the Count of Anjou.*

idea was worth trying. King Henry entrusted the somewhat delicate process of diplomatic bargaining to Thomas Becket. Becket would go to France and prepare the way for a meeting between Louis and Henry later in the year to finalize the deal. It must be remembered that in the Middle Ages, marriage contracts between royal houses were frequently made. It was a common way of forming political alliances.

During this journey to France, Becket astounded the French with his overwhelming display of wealth and luxury. Accompanying him on his journey were 200 men on horseback. They were all dressed in finely tailored new clothes. There were also hundreds of other servants, clerks, secretaries, cooks, butlers, and various officials. Becket's own personal collection of eight carriages, each drawn by five gigantic horses, contained things that were deliberately designed to impress his French hosts.

There were casks of beer, fine foods, gold and silver cups, spoons, and knives (forks hadn't yet been invented). Huge dogs guarded each vehicle. To add an exotic touch, a long-tailed monkey rode on the back of every packhorse. It was little wonder that the French peasants who watched this extraordinary stream of Englishmen passing through their villages were utterly amazed by what they saw.

This picture from the Bayeux Tapestry shows knights on horseback charging against foot soldiers. The tapestry was made by Norman embroiderers in the eleventh century. It is 230 feet (70 meters) long and depicts the story of how William the Conqueror defeated England at the Battle of Hastings in 1066. Underneath the main action is a separate frieze, showing the dead and wounded. The soldiers are wearing chain-mail armor, which is made from small pieces of iron that are linked together like a chain. Becket would have worn this kind of armor.

The citizens of Paris were even more astonished. When Becket stayed in their city, he was able to feed 1,000 guests for days. This display of generosity was deliberately calculated to impress his French hosts. In fact, when Henry came later to meet Louis, the

marriage arrangements were completed without difficulty. This way, Henry was able to claim the Vexin.

BECKET FIGHTS IN ARMOR ON BEHALF OF HENRY

The following year, in 1159, Becket revealed another side of his character. The friendship between Henry and Louis quickly faded. This was because a dangerous situation had developed in which Henry was fighting to claim the province of Toulouse in the south of France on behalf of his wife, Eleanor.

Eleanor was demanding that Count Raymond, the ruler of Toulouse, acknowledge that he owed his position to her as her vassal (subordinate). King Henry was supporting her in this claim. However, Count Raymond refused to do this. He was asking Louis to help him as he defended himself against Henry. This kind of quarrel may seem rather con-fused and unimportant, but at the time, the issue was sensitive and led to a campaign of open warfare.

Henry led a large army south to Toulouse. Naturally, Becket was required to accompany him. Although he had never taken part in a war, Becket was determined to show how skilled he was. He had learned much about fighting in his boyhood at Pevensey Castle. There were many skirmishes in which Becket displayed remarkable ability in horsemanship and the handling of weapons.

The confrontation between Louis and Henry had no satisfactory outcome for either side. Eventually, Henry went north, leaving Becket in charge of a large troop of men. Becket continued to show his military expertise. Splendidly dressed in full armor, he led his men in fighting the French army. One of Becket's memorable military exploits probably occurred when he charged at full gallop against a well-known French knight, Engelram de Trie. This knight had a considerable reputation as a heroic warrior. However, Becket was successful in knocking him off his horse, which he then led away in triumph.

THE DEATH OF ARCHBISHOP THEOBALD

Theobald, the aging archbishop of Canterbury, had brought Becket into his household when he was a very young man. Now he watched Becket change from a humble clerk to the most spectacularly wealthy and powerful man in England. He was bitterly disappointed with Becket. The archbishop had wanted to place a loyal churchman beside the king to guide him in his reign. Instead, he saw Becket becoming more and more worldly. Worse still, Becket was neglecting all his duties as archdeacon of Canterbury—and he frequently supported the king against the church whenever disputes came up.

Theobald's health was declining. He longed to see Becket and talk to him face-to-face. He wanted to tell him how disappointed he was that Becket had become so caught up in state business that he was neglecting his duties in Canterbury. As he lay dying, Theobald wrote letter after letter begging Becket to visit him. However, Becket always wrote back with excuses. Theobald became angry and pointed out to Becket that he owed him everything. In addition, he was archbishop, and Becket owed him loyalty and obedience. Becket's excuse was that his first duty was to the king.

Sadly, Becket never did visit Theobald in his final sickness. The elderly man died in April 1161 without a chance to speak to Becket. His death left the church in England without a leader. Clearly, King Henry needed to find the best person possible to fill the vacancy. He needed someone who would fit in with his ways and a person who would support his plans for the country. He wanted someone he could trust—if possible, a friend.

Thomas Becket occurred to him immediately, but he did not make any appointment for more than a year. Perhaps he realized that Becket would not be a welcome choice by many churchmen. One person who would be deeply offended if Becket became archbishop was Gilbert Foliot, the bishop of Hereford. He was a man of great learning and holiness. He was also a practical man who was knowledgeable about political affairs. He did not disguise the fact that he hoped the king might choose him to be the new archbishop.

At last, Henry made his decision. He privately told Becket that he intended to appoint him as the new archbishop of Canterbury. At first, Becket was extremely reluctant to accept the post. He was enjoying the chancellorship, and the change in becoming archbishop would present difficulties of divided loyalties. He is said to have warned Henry that he would not allow any interference in church matters. However, this may well be a story that was made up in later years. Nevertheless, he allowed his name to be put forward for election, first by the monks of

This photo shows the south side of Canterbury Cathedral. Christianity was brought to southern England by Saint Augustine in AD 597. He founded a church and monastery on the present site and was made the first archbishop. This cathedral, which was built over many centuries, was completed in the late fourteenth century. Thomas Becket was archbishop from 1162 to 1170. Traditionally, the archbishop of Canterbury is the leader of the English Christian Church.

Canterbury and then by a larger body of all the leading nobles and churchmen. Everyone knew that the king wanted Becket in the position. The election was just a formality. All the same, Gilbert Foliot had the courage to speak out against Becket. He stated that Becket had harmed the church by demanding money from its funds to help pay for his campaign in Toulouse. The church owned much property and land. It gained its income from renting those possessions.

Ultimately, since Foliot was the only one to dis-agree with the election of Becket, he was ignored. That left only one more arrangement to be made. Becket had to be ordained a priest. It is incredible to think that until the time that he was about to become archbishop, Becket had not yet been given the authority of a priest. However, this matter was soon fixed. On June 2, 1162, Becket was received into the priesthood. The next day, he presented himself at Canterbury Cathedral to be consecrated as the fortieth archbishop of Canterbury. Tears of emotion streamed down his face as he thought of the future and the awesome responsibility of serving God.

Becket as Archbishop of Canterbury

No one could have imagined the dramatic change that took place in Thomas Becket's personality and lifestyle immediately after he became archbishop of Canterbury. Overnight, he seemed to have become a different man.

Instead of wearing the most expensive clothes, he now wore the dark habit of a monk, with an uncomfortably rough shirt next to his skin. In the Middle Ages, it was considered a sign of great holiness to dress like this. Also, instead of eating and drinking the finest foods and wines, Becket hardly ate enough to keep himself alive. He drank only water. During these sparse meals, he constantly listened to readings from holy books.

Everything he did emphasized the fact that he was committed to a religious way of life—or at least, the extreme way in which religion was

This is a nineteenth-century artist's impression of Becket washing the feet of beggars who have come to Canterbury Cathedral. This act is similar to Jesus Christ's washing the feet of his followers, which showed humility and a willingness to serve the very poor. Today, some priests symbolically wash the feet of the members of their church.

often practiced in the Middle Ages.

In imitation of Christ's action in washing the feet of his disciples, every day Becket washed the feet of at least a dozen poor men. At night, he prayed for hours on end instead of sleeping. He frequently stripped to the waist and asked to be whipped, to show how sorry he was for everything he had done wrong in the past.

Naturally, most people who witnessed this extraordinary transformation were amazed. In fact, they could hardly believe what they saw. However, Gilbert Foliot, Becket's rival and opponent, took a rather more scornful view. As quoted in *Materials for a History of Thomas Becket, Archbishop of Canterbury*, by J. C. Robertson and J. B. Sheppard, he remarked to his friends: "It seems that the King has wrought [created] a miracle! He has created an Archbishop out of a soldier and a man of the world!"

As for King Henry, he was as astonished as everyone else. This change was unexpected. Even more unexpected was Becket's first act on becoming the archbishop. He returned the Great Seal to Henry and resigned his position as king's chancellor. This came as an unwelcome surprise to Henry. The whole point of making Becket the archbishop was to combine the two great offices in one man. King Henry's plan was to gain influence over the church, using Becket as his friend and ally. Becket had never given any hint that he would refuse to combine the two jobs. It was obvious that from then on, there would be a more distant relationship between the two men.

TROUBLE FOR THE ARCHBISHOP AT WESTMINSTER

Becket's dramatic display of religious behavior was soon followed by a sharp attention to church affairs. He had shown great energy and skill as chancellor. Now, he used this energy to win back all the lands and property that had been wrongly taken from the

This is a photo of Rochester Castle in Kent. This castle was built by Archbishop William de Corbeil in 1127. William was the archbishop before Theobald and had crowned King Stephen. The castle, therefore, belonged to the church, but Henry II claimed it for himself. Not surprisingly, Becket was determined to claim it back for the church.

church by William the Conqueror. Becket employed lawyers to help him investigate what he believed was illegally owned property. William the Conqueror had seized lands belonging to the church and had given them to his Norman lords. Becket was determined to have these properties restored to the church. For example, he demanded that Roger de Clare (who was

Earl of Hertford and a powerful Norman baron) give up his home, Tonbridge Castle. Becket claimed that this castle was church property. He also demanded that the king give up Rochester Castle, near London, and hand it back to the church.

Becket then quarreled with the king over other matters. He resisted any attempt by Henry to interfere with his running the church. A major cause for disagreement was over the way in which clergy who had committed crimes should be tried and punished. The difficulty lay in the fact that in England there were two kinds of courts for trying criminals: the royal courts and the church courts. Any criminal who was a member of the clergy was supposed to be tried by the church courts. However, Henry was angry that many churchmen were not being properly punished. It was well known that the church courts gave easy sentences or even let clergy off without any punishment at all.

From King Henry's point of view, there were too many clergy in "minor orders"—in other words, they were not fully priests because their roles in the church were limited. However, the fact that they were somehow attached to the church gave them the excuse not to be tried in the royal courts. This state of affairs was not satisfactory to Henry. Accordingly, in 1163, he called a meeting of senior churchmen to a council in Westminster to discuss his plans for reform. At this meeting, Henry's suggestions included sacking (or firing) these criminals from their jobs so that they could not claim to be clergy. Then they could be brought before the royal courts just like anyone else. It seemed a fair compromise, and many bishops were prepared to agree.

Becket, however, flatly refused to have anything to do with the king's proposals. He also persuaded the bishops that it would be wrong to give in. When the king asked Becket whether he was prepared to observe the ancient customs and laws of the country, Becket's reply was carefully phrased.

According to records kept at the time, and quoted in *Materials for a History of Thomas Becket, Archbishop of Canterbury*, by J. C. Robertson and J. B. Sheppard, he said that he would certainly observe all those laws, "saving the privileges of my order." This curious wording meant that, as a priest, he reserved the right not to obey or observe anything that he thought was against church principles. In fact, he was saying that he would obey the king only when it pleased him to do so. Each bishop except one followed Becket's example, using exactly the same words. Needless to say, Henry was furious and left the meeting without a word. Later that day, Becket received an abrupt message from the king demanding that he give up all the property he still held from the time when he was chancellor. Clearly, the two men were on a collision course.

MORE TROUBLE FOR THE ARCHBISHOP AT CLARENDON

During the following months, Henry busied himself by speaking to all the bishops individually. In doing so, he managed to win them over to his point of view. Privately, the bishops told him that they were prepared to accept the ancient customs of England without adding the offensive phrase "saving the privileges of my order." Henry argued that the ancient customs and laws of England did not include the right of the church to try criminals. He explained that all he was doing was bringing back traditions of justice that had been observed for centuries.

A group of bishops then went to Becket to beg him not to be stubborn. Eventually, after much persuasion, Becket actually agreed to withdraw the sensitive phrase. When he learned about this, Henry announced that he wanted Becket and the bishops to come to a meeting of the Great Council at his royal palace at Clarendon, near Salisbury. It was his desire that the whole matter be formally and publicly discussed. In that way, he was hopeful that an agreement between church and state could be reached.

A CLASH OF PERSONALITIES AT THE COUNCIL OF CLARENDON

The meeting at Clarendon took place in January 1164. For the meeting, Henry had prepared a document known as the Constitutions of Clarendon. It contained all the legal points that he wanted Becket and the bishops to agree to. There were sixteen points that, Henry claimed, related to the ancient laws of England. However, they were also about the position of the clergy with regard to the law of the land. When Becket saw that these were designed to limit the liberties of his clergy, he immediately declared that the constitutions were an outrage. To allow a mere royal court to punish a member of the church was like laying hands on Christ himself. "Touch not mine anointed!" were his crucial words, as he quoted from the Bible.

The argument between the king and archbishop went on and on. Some bishops tried to persuade

"TOUCH NOT MINE ANOINTED"

This dramatic phrase is a quotation from the Bible and is found in Psalm 105, verse 15. The word "anointed" refers to the biblical practice of pouring holy oil over priests and kings as a symbol of their sacred position. By saying this, Becket was hoping to shock Henry into realizing that the Bible itself could be quoted against him.

Becket to be more flexible. They pointed out that the king might well lose all patience with them and their lives could be in danger. Leading barons also begged the archbishop to try to arrive at a compromise. More bishops were brought in as peacemakers, but Becket still remained firmly opposed to the king.

Finally, on the third day of the conference, just as the bishops were discussing what to do next, they were suddenly surprised. The doors of the room where they were meeting burst open and armed soldiers stormed in, waving their swords and shouting. They threatened the bishops by declaring that they were prepared to use their weapons in any way the king might command. No one knows whether Henry himself had sent these soldiers or whether they had decided to act on their own initiative.

Afterward, Becket left the room for a short while. When he returned, he astounded the bishops by announcing that he had decided to give in to Henry and accept the constitutions just as the king wanted. Later that day, at the meeting of the Great Council, Becket went even further. He ordered all his bishops to make a formal declaration of acceptance. Shocked and amazed at their leader's sudden change of mind, they had no option but to obey him. What they said behind Becket's back can only be guessed. However, a few years later, in a letter to Becket himself, Gilbert Foliot wrote, "We had never expected that the Lord's disciple would be so easily turned aside."

Becket returned to Canterbury. His conscience was telling him that he had betrayed himself, his church, and his God. Little wonder that, once again, tears again streamed down his face—but this time they were tears of shame.

BECKET CONTINUES TO DEFY THE KING

CHAPTER 5

Although Becket had agreed to accept the Constitutions of Clarendon, he refused to attach his seal to them. Furthermore, he did not put his agreement in writing. Instead, he said that an archbishop's word was as good as an oath. However, he obtained a copy of the Constitutions of Clarendon. This he intended to take to the pope in person and make his complaint about Henry's demands. Meanwhile, Becket wrote to the pope asking forgiveness for the weakness he had shown in agreeing to the constitutions. He received a sympathetic reply from the pope.

Twice, Becket tried to sail to France to make the journey to Rome. The first time, the weather was bad. The second time, the sailors refused to go out to sea. They had recognized the

This is a stained-glass window in the Cathedral of Saint Étienne. This scene shows Becket returning to England after setting sail from Wissant on the French coast. The Cathedral of Saint Étienne in France contains a window that tells the story of the life of Thomas Becket.

archbishop and knew that the king would be angry if they accepted Becket as a passenger. Meanwhile, relations between Henry and Becket became even more tense. Becket openly defied the king. Henry had summoned him to appear in a royal court of law to answer a case that was being brought against Becket by a man named John Marshall. The details of the case are not important, but Henry was angry when Becket refused to attend this court. It was his duty to appear. By not doing so, he was deliberately breaking his oath of obedience to the king. Furious with Becket, Henry commanded him to appear at another meeting of the Great Council. This meeting was to be held in Northampton, a town in central England, in October 1164.

THE COUNCIL OF NORTHAMPTON

The Council of Northampton was deliberately planned by Henry to crush Becket completely. The most important men of the church and the greatest noblemen of England were present. Becket was formally charged with contempt of the king by failing to appear at his royal court of law. The case was discussed, and when Becket was found guilty,

Henry declared that Becket must lose everything he still possessed. It was an extremely heavy sentence, but the king did not stop at that. On the following day, he charged Becket with a number of other acts of misconduct that, according to Henry, he had committed during the time that he was chancellor.

The king claimed that Becket had kept money for himself instead of handing it over to the royal treasury. For example, Henry said that as warden of the castles at Eye and Berkhamstead, Becket had pocketed the rent. In response to the accusation, Becket said that he had spent the money in making repairs to the castles, along with the Tower of London. To this, Henry replied that he had never asked for the repairs. He pressed Becket to return the sum of 300 pounds to him. This was an enormous sum in those days. And, of course, Becket had just lost everything he owned, so he couldn't possibly pay.

BECKET WALKS OUT ON THE KING

Henry went even further and demanded to see all the accounts of every abbey and diocese during Becket's time as chancellor. This would require

weeks of preparation. Becket promised he would do so, if he were given enough time. But Henry then demanded that Becket provide sureties (men willing to promise to pay all this money on Becket's behalf). Of course, the sums of money involved were so large that no one could be found to promise such amounts. It was becoming obvious that Henry was deliberately making Becket's life extremely difficult.

For Becket, the strain and anxiety must have been considerable. For a few days, he was ill. However, he promised the king that he would get up from his sickbed and appear before him to answer all the charges. When he did so, three days later, Becket arrived in a most dramatic manner. He was barefoot, and he solemnly carried a large silver cross. Henry asked the bishops to declare that Becket was in the wrong. However, they were

This aerial photo of the Tower of London clearly shows the large central castle, which is known as the White Tower. William the Conqueror began its construction shortly after the Battle of Hastings. Later kings built the outer wall and the towers at intervals along it. In Becket's time, this outer wall did not exist, but the White Tower (so called because it was whitewashed at that period of time) was one of the main residences of the kings of England.

THE PUNISHMENT OF EXCOMMUNICATION

The worst punishment that a Catholic priest could give was that of excommunication. This means banishment from the church and from the approval of God. Those who were excommunicated could not attend any church

This is an illuminated manuscript page that shows King John and his two dogs. King John, who was born in Oxford on December 24, 1167, and who died at Newark Castle on October 19, 1216, was king of England from 1199 to 1216. This image is from the Anglo-Norman Chronicle, which was written in French verse by Peter Langtoft in the first quarter of the fourteenth century. Langtoft was a canon of the Augustinian priory at Brindlington in the north of England.

services or make confession. Neither could they receive pardon for their sins. Excommunication was fairly common in the Middle Ages. On occasion, whole nations were excommunicated. This was called being "placed under an interdict." For example, England was placed under an interdict for more than five years during the reign of King John (1199–1216), who refused to accept the pope's choice of candidate for archbishop of Canterbury.

extremely reluctant to condemn the archbishop, especially because Becket told them that by doing so they would be breaking their oath of obedience to him. When it was Becket's turn to speak, he confirmed that he had forbidden the bishops to make any judgment on him. According to John of Salisbury (as noted in *Materials for a History of Thomas Becket*), he ended his speech by saying, "I place myself and the Church of Canterbury under the protection of God and the Pope."

After this, Henry asked the barons to sentence Becket. However, they were reluctant to act. They were afraid that Becket would excommunicate them

This is an illuminated manuscript page showing a conversation taking place between King Henry II of England and Thomas Becket, archbishop of Canterbury. This English manuscript dates from the first quarter of the fourteenth century.

if they did so. This meant that they would be formally excluded from the church and therefore would be sent to hell after their deaths. Then the king ordered that the Earl of Leicester sentence him. When he heard this, Becket immediately began protesting loudly, saying that he had not been given a proper trial. He refused to listen to anything the earl might say. Still carrying the cross, Becket walked out of the room, amid jeers and shouts of "Traitor!" from the barons.

BECKET IN FRANCE

Knowing that his life was in danger if he remained in England, Becket went to a nearby abbey in Northampton. As soon as he could, he made his way to the coast. Then, accompanied by only a few companions, he crossed over to France in a dangerously small boat. This was secretly done during the night, regardless of the extremely bad, stormy weather.

When Henry heard the news that Becket had escaped to France, he wrote to King Louis of France and asked him not to give his "former Archbishop" any aid or a place to live. However, Louis was very pleased to provide Becket with hospitality. This was partly to annoy Henry and partly because he sincerely believed that Henry had no power over any churchman. With Louis's help, Becket set off to see the pope.

Curiously, at this time, there were two popes, and each claimed to be the "real" one. In 1159, Pope Alexander III had been driven out of Rome by a rival who called himself Pope Victor IV. However, both King Louis and Becket supported Alexander as the proper pope. Accordingly, Becket went to see Pope Alexander III, who was then living at Sens in France, about 65 miles (104 kilometers) southeast of Paris. He arrived in magnificent style with a large company of supporters, thanks to the generosity of King Louis.

Becket showed his copy of the Constitutions of Clarendon to the pope, who immediately declared them unacceptable to the church. Although he reprimanded Becket for having

This illuminated manuscript page from *Les Grandes Chroniques de France* (The Great Chronicles of France, circa 1335 to 1340) shows King Louis receiving the bishop of Clermont. The bishop, who is wearing his mitre (a bishop's hat) is shown to be kneeling to the king, indicating that he accepts his authority.

accepted them, he realized the difficult situation he had been in. Nevertheless, Pope Alexander was reluctant to be harsh on King Henry. The king had supported him in the past. Because of this and because his position as pope was still not secure, he was anxious to avoid making an enemy of Henry. His sympathy with Becket was carefully expressed, so as to avoid offending the king.

The next day, Becket once again met with the pope and his cardinals. To everyone's surprise, Becket began the meeting by offering to resign as archbishop. He declared that he no longer had the strength to carry on. Naturally, the pope was taken aback and asked Becket to leave the room while he discussed the situation. Then, calling him back, he told Becket that under no circumstances would he allow him to resign. He then confirmed Becket's position as archbishop. This, of course, would be a setback to Henry, who would have dearly liked to have gotten rid of him.

However, with cunning diplomacy, Pope Alexander prevented Becket from returning to England. He ordered him to live the life of a humble monk in the French monastery of Pontigny, about 30 miles (48 km) southeast of Sens. He added that it would do Becket good to submit to such a simple lifestyle.

In December 1164, Becket arrived at Pontigny and began a life of exile that was to last for almost five years. Despite everything that had happened, he was still the archbishop of Canterbury.

THE DISPUTE CONTINUES

The awkward situation between King Henry and Thomas Becket needed to be resolved. However, the years dragged on until, eventually, Henry felt he had to somehow break the deadlock. Accordingly, a meeting was arranged in January 1169 at Montmirail in northern France. As always, many of the most important nobles and churchmen were present. Even King Louis of France came to witness the proceedings.

Arguments about the ancient customs of England were discussed yet again. However, Becket still wanted to retain the phrase "saving my order," which had infuriated Henry at Clarendon and Northampton. Eventually, Becket was persuaded to give up this phrase. A formal ceremony of reconciliation was arranged, and the two kings sat waiting for Becket to make his

This image is from a stained-glass window in the cathedral of the city of Saint Étienne in central France. It illustrates the reconciliation of Thomas Becket with King Henry II in the presence of Louis VII of France. The stained glass dates from the thirteenth century and is part of a very large window that depicts scenes of the life of Thomas Becket.

entrance. However, just as he was making his way into the meeting hall, Becket encountered one of his closest supporters, Herbert of Bosham.

Herbert, who was fanatically opposed to any form of compromise, pressed forward through the crowd and (according to John of Salisbury, Becket's personal secretary) whispered, "Be on your guard, my Lord! If you give up the phrase 'saving the honor of God' you will bitterly regret it." Becket did not reply but went forward to meet Henry and knelt down before him. Henry graciously took his hand and raised Becket to his feet.

It was time for Becket to speak. He acknowledged that he had been the cause of much trouble, saying, "I cast [throw] myself on your mercy and on your judgement." There was a pause. Then, in defiance of the king, he added: "Saving the honor of God!" This phrase, of course, meant that whatever the king might order him to do, he would obey him only if he, Becket, decided that it was also the will of God. Put briefly, it meant that he did not accept the authority of the king. Everyone present was shocked and amazed. Henry was beside himself with rage. As the meeting broke up in confusion, King Louis, astonished by Becket's stubbornness, asked, "My Lord, are you trying to be more than a saint?" It is clear that Louis believed that Becket had overstepped the limits of his position.

BECKET EXCOMMUNICATES BISHOPS AND NOBLES

King Henry and many of the bishops and political leaders were desperately looking to the pope to help solve the difficulties with Becket. This made Becket very angry at what he believed to be their interference.

From France, he declared a sentence of excommunication on a group of English bishops and nobles who were supporting Henry's attempts at compromise. He even threatened to excommunicate the king and put England under an interdict. This would mean that no church services could be held throughout the land, including baptisms, marriages, or even funerals. Fortunately for the English church, the pope refused to confirm these excommunications.

In November 1169, yet another meeting was arranged between Henry and Becket. This one was to take place at Montmartre, in the north of Paris. At this meeting, Henry actually offered to withdraw his demands about "ancient laws of England." There were many conditions and qualifications. At the end of the negotiations, it still wasn't quite clear what had been agreed upon. However, it seemed that Henry was offering to reinstate Becket as archbishop and make some form of recompense for salaries lost during his exile.

An agreement was just in sight when Becket demanded a kiss of peace. In the Middle Ages, this gesture of a kiss was customarily exchanged when a bargain was made. Henry then became stubborn and declared that he could not make the kiss of peace because he had sworn on oath never to do so with Becket. As might be expected, Becket then refused to continue with the agreements that seemed to have been made.

However, both men were tired of conflict. Later in the year, in July 1170, a form of peace was made between them at a quiet meeting in an open field at Fréteval in France. The agreement was deliberately vague to avoid further arguments, so many issues were still left unresolved. It was agreed, however, that Becket would return to Canterbury in the autumn of that year.

THE CORONATION OF HENRY THE YOUNG KING

Just before the meeting at Fréteval, Henry had arranged for his eldest son and heir, also called Henry, to be crowned king in Westminster Abbey. To have the successor crowned while the reigning king still lived was a curious custom. It was not intended to give any

This image shows the wedding of Philip Augustus, king of France, to Isabella of Hennegau in 1180. It is from a French book illumination that dates back to the second half of the fifteenth century. The elaborate clothing that they are dressed in is very similar to what would have been worn at a coronation such as Henry's.

N l'an de nre seigneur
mil cent soixante
dix et noef fut

vngs traitie de mariage entre
phelippe le roy de france et ysa
bel fille du conte bauduin

kingly power to the heir. The freshly crowned sixteen-year-old was known as Henry the Young King. In theory, he was king of England, just as his father was, but at such a young age, Henry was king in name only.

Becket was furious that this coronation had taken place. In England, only the archbishop of Canterbury had the power to crown a king. Becket had written from France to all the bishops forbidding them to take part in any coronation service. He was insulted because he had not been asked to crown the young king himself. He was furious with three men in particular who had taken part in crowning the young king—Roger, archbishop of York; Gilbert Foliot, bishop of London; and Joscelin, bishop of Salisbury. Because of their deliberate disobedience, Becket sent letters of excommunication to the two bishops and the archbishop of York, suspending them from their duties. He believed that all of them had sinned against God and against him.

BECKET RETURNS TO CANTERBURY

Becket had reached a peaceful agreement with Henry at Fréteval. He returned to Canterbury at the beginning of December 1170. He was still annoyed with the three rebellious bishops. However, he was pleased to be home again, and the people of Canterbury welcomed him with great joy. Music could be heard throughout the cathedral, and trumpeters played as he made his entrance. It had been six years since Becket had seen his friends, and he gave each monk a kiss of greeting.

The next day, he was met by officials from the king. They demanded that the archbishop of York and the two bishops who had taken part in the young king's coronation be pardoned and the sentences of excommunication withdrawn. This posed a problem for Becket. He didn't want to seem weak or to give in to the king. He replied that he would have to ask for the pope's opinion. Becket realized that King Henry was determined to have his own way. He also sensed that he was likely to be in danger if this dispute over the bishops continued to anger the king.

Meanwhile, the archbishop of York and the two other bishops had crossed the English Channel to meet the king, who was spending Christmas near Bayeux. They complained about their excommunication and the way Becket was behaving. They also told the king that he would never have any peace as long as Becket was alive.

Back in Canterbury, Becket used the occasion of his Christmas Day service in the cathedral to preach an extraordinarily dramatic sermon. He spoke of his

This seal of Canterbury Cathedral shows the old Romanesque cathedral with weather vanes, which would have been familiar to Becket.

own death and told his congregation that this would take place soon. He also spoke of possible martyrdom. Then, he proceeded to pass sentences of excommunication on six more people who had displeased him in various ways. Finally, he confirmed the excommunication he had already passed on the archbishop of York and the bishops of London and Salisbury.

Reaching a tremendously theatrical ending to his sermon, Becket solemnly cursed the disobedient bishops. He said that he wanted to blot out their memory from his mind. He picked up lighted candles and hurled them to the ground to show how angry he was with them.

There are reliable eyewitness accounts of this astonishing outburst from two monks: Gervase of Canterbury and Becket's own secretary, John of Salisbury. Both of these men wrote detailed descriptions of Becket's life and were good, reliable historians.

News of Thomas Becket's powerfully worded sermon quickly reached King Henry in France. His reaction soon became famous throughout Europe.

An undated engraving of King Henry II (1133–1189). This is an artist's impression, which cannot be taken as a true likeness. However, King Henry is shown wearing a typical medieval royal crown. At Christmas, Easter, and Whitsun, English kings would hold special "crown-wearing" ceremonies to remind their subjects of their power and authority.

Whether he really said these words, no one will ever know. However, historic records claim that he burst out with uncontrolled anger, shouting to everyone within hearing distance: "Will nobody rid me of this turbulent priest?"

Four of his knights decided to carry out his wishes immediately.

MURDER IN THE CATHEDRAL

Among those who heard Henry's outburst against Becket were four knights: Reginald FitzUrse, William de Tracy, Hugh de Morville, and Richard Brito. They decided to take matters into their own hands and do what the king seemed to want—get rid of Becket. They left the king's household immediately, each traveling by a different route. They met up with one another on December 28, 1170, at Saltwood Castle in Kent.

Meanwhile, Henry had learned of their departure. Realizing what they probably intended to do, he sent three officials after the knights to bring them back. However, it was too late. The four knights arrived in Canterbury on Friday, December 29, late in the afternoon. They made enquiries about where they could find the archbishop and learned that

Becket was dining in a building near the cathedral. Night was already beginning to fall when they burst into the room where Becket had just finished his meal. They roughly pushed their way through into a smaller room where Becket was seated, talking to one of the monks.

Fortunately for later historians, the events that followed were witnessed by one of the finest scholars of the age, John of Salisbury. He wrote many works of history in addition to letters that contain vivid descriptions and accounts of the times. The following conversations were taken from John of Salisbury's own eyewitness account.

When the knights entered the room where Becket was sitting, Becket greeted them politely with God's blessing. "God help you, rather," they replied. At that moment, Becket realized why they had come. The knights told him they had brought a message from the king. They asked Becket whether he would prefer to hear it privately or in public. "In public," replied Becket. Then he called for monks and attendants to enter the room. Reginald FitzUrse then accused Becket of breaking the peace that had been made with the king. He added that Becket had insulted King Henry by excommunicating the bishops who had crowned his son. When

FitzUrse demanded that Becket withdraw the sentences of excommunication, Becket told him that this was a matter for the pope.

"It is by your doing that they were sentenced," FitzUrse replied. "You must absolve [pardon] them!" When Becket refused, the knights started threatening him. They told him that he was insulting King Henry. Becket became angry and replied: "If anyone breaks the laws of the Church, I will not spare him—no matter who he may be." The knights took this as a challenge. "Do you dare to threaten us? Be careful of what you say, for your life is in danger."

A DREADFUL DEED COMMITTED IN THE CATHEDRAL

Becket was silent for a while before he spoke. "I see murder in your faces. Have you come to kill me?" he asked. "I tell you that if all the swords in England were pointing at my head, you would never make me betray either God or the Pope. I am at least as ready to face martyrdom as you are to strike."

The knights then left the room with Becket calling angrily after them. John of Salisbury spoke to Becket and asked: "Why did you have to be so

This image, from a thirteenth-century illuminated manuscript, illustrates the assassination of Thomas Becket in Canterbury Cathedral on December 29, 1170. Becket's mitre is shown falling to the ground. It may be that the artist was illustrating the moment before the top of Becket's head was sliced open.

provocative [make them angry]? You could have discussed things with them more peacefully." He added, "We are sinners, and not yet prepared to die. I don't see anyone here, except you, who actually wants to die." To this, Becket replied, "I know well enough what I must do."

By now, Becket's companions were thoroughly alarmed. The terrified monks begged him to hide inside the cathedral. "Never," Becket replied. However, at their desperate pleading, he finally gave in. They physically pushed and pulled him to make him walk faster. Meanwhile, the knights had put on their armor and were making their way into the cathedral, where an evening service had just been held.

By then, it was five o'clock. As the cathedral was lit by only a few candles, it was bathed in darkness. Becket was standing between two altars when the knights made their entrance. "Where is the traitor?" they shouted. Becket called out, "Here I am. No traitor, but a priest of God. What do you want of me?" he asked.

"We want your death!" was the reply.

The final moment had come. As Becket folded his hands in prayer, FitzUrse landed the first blow, swinging his heavy sword and slicing the top of Becket's scalp from his head. Edward Grim, a monk who had stayed with Becket, was injured on the arm by the same blow. After that, the knights all joined in, showering blows upon the archbishop, who lay bleeding on the ground. One of the knights put his foot on Becket's neck, pushed his sword into Becket's head, and scooped out his brains, spilling them onto the cathedral floor. "The traitor will not rise again," he said.

KING HENRY'S EMBARRASSMENT AND GRIEF

When Henry heard the news of Becket's murder, he was stunned with grief. He remained shut up in his private room for three days. In fact, for almost six weeks, he seemed paralyzed with shock. He was desperately sorry that he had been the cause of Becket's death. He had lost an archbishop of great distinction and a former friend. The two men had been linked together as either friends or enemies for many years. Henry could not forgive himself for what had happened.

Apart from the loss of a friend, Henry had to deal with the fact that his own political reputation was ruined. He realized that this horrific death would turn Becket into a martyr, while he would be seen as a murderer. By his death, Becket had triumphed. The great battle between church and state, waged with such passion during Becket's time as archbishop, was over and Becket had won.

Obviously, Henry had to deal with a very serious situation. He wrote to the pope, expressing his sorrow and explaining that it had not been his intention to kill Becket. The whole of Europe was horrified at what had happened. It was not just a murder but also a monstrous sacrilege: Becket was not merely a victim, but a holy saint. Indeed, within a few days of his death, miracles were being recorded by his grave. People were claiming to be cured of their illnesses by praying at the site of his murder.

THE POLITICAL CONSEQUENCES OF BECKET'S DEATH

Pope Alexander, naturally, was deeply shocked at Becket's death and pronounced sentences of excommunication on all who had been involved in the crime. Henry himself was forbidden to enter a church until he had been properly absolved—that is, officially pardoned by the church for his part in the event, unintentional though it might have been.

The ceremony at which Henry was pardoned came seventeen months later, at the cathedral of

Avranches, in northern France, on May 21, 1172. Before the actual ceremony, however, Pope Alexander took the opportunity to punish Henry and extract several promises from him. First, the pope demanded that Henry provide 200 knights to fight the Muslims in Palestine and he was to keep them there for a year. Second, Henry himself was to go to fight in a crusade. The pope also demanded that Henry withdraw all the laws that he had introduced that were in any way harmful to the church. As well, he was made to give to the church all goods and property that had been confiscated from Becket while he was in exile. Finally, and certainly most important of all, Henry was to agree that the royal courts had no power to try any member of the clergy and that only the church courts could do this. This, of course, had been a major point of disagreement with Becket. It was a tremendous victory for the church.

After all these demands were agreed upon by Henry, the great service was held in Avranches Cathedral. Henry placed his hand on the Bible and solemnly swore that he had never intended the archbishop's death and that he had been deeply saddened by what had happened. Henry was then led outside the cathedral and, kneeling on the ground, he received absolution. This cathedral no longer exists,

This is the site of the murder of Thomas Becket. The stone inscription in Canterbury Cathedral reads, "In this place hallowed [made holy] by the martyrdom of St. Thomas Pope John Paul II and Robert Runcie Archbishop of Canterbury knelt together in prayer May 29, 1982."

but to this day, a stone slab marks the spot where Henry knelt and received the church's pardon.

KING HENRY GOES TO CANTERBURY TO BE BEATEN BY THE MONKS

Two years after this ceremony in Avranches, Henry decided to make a dramatic gesture of penitence in Canterbury itself, to show everyone there how deeply he felt. He went to Canterbury on June 12, 1174, but stopped three miles (almost five km) outside the city.

Then, barefoot and wearing nothing but a shirt, he walked to the cathedral. He knelt to pray at the cathedral porch and then, with his feet bleeding from cuts made by the rough, stony road, he made his way to the spot where the murder had taken place. He then kissed the stones where Becket had fallen.

After a ceremony of penitence and absolution he submitted to being beaten. He suffered three strokes from each of the eight monks, and five strokes from each of the various bishops and abbots. Still muddy and unwashed, he then spent the whole of the night in the cathedral crypt, fasting and praying, and shivering with cold.

BECKET IN HISTORY

Miracles were believed to have occurred at Becket's grave within days of his death. Blindness, illnesses, accidents to limbs: Becket's apparent power to cure all ailments seemed limitless. Pope Alexander canonized Becket (that is, made him a saint) in 1173, less than three years after he had been murdered. Ordinary people regarded him as a saint from the day of his martyrdom. Within ten years of his death, no fewer than 703 miracles were recorded by the monks at Canterbury Cathedral.

This reliquary casket from Limoges, France, depicts the murder and burial of Thomas Becket. This scene is visible on the top of the enameled box. A reliquary is a small container in which a precious object is kept—usually a memento of a saint, or even a bone or part of a body.

Over the next 365 years, thousands more miracles were believed to have taken place. Representations of Becket's martyrdom in books, stained-glass windows, and carvings were made throughout Europe. In England, eighty churches were dedicated to Saint Thomas of Canterbury. It is impossible to exaggerate how popular and important Saint Thomas became to English people throughout the next three and a half centuries. His shrine in Canterbury Cathedral attracted hundreds of thousands of pilgrims from all parts of Europe. Rather gruesomely,

THE CANTERBURY TALES

Two centuries after Becket's death, a famous English poet, Geoffrey Chaucer, wrote about a group of about twenty pilgrims traveling from London to Saint Thomas Becket's shrine in Canterbury. Chaucer imagined that each pilgrim agreed to tell a story to entertain the others as they rode their horses along the way. Geoffrey Chaucer's *Canterbury Tales* are the most famous set of English poems written in the Middle Ages. They give a good description of what these pilgrimages were like. The pilgrims represented all ranks of society, from knights to humble cooks.

This is a fifteenth-century English manuscript illumination showing Geoffrey Chaucer. Chaucer, a very famous English poet, wrote The Canterbury Tales. *These tales provide an amusing and detailed view of medieval society.*

Becket's skull, with its severed top, was displayed in a special golden casket shaped like Becket's own head.

Two routes through the English countryside to Canterbury became known as the Pilgrims' Way, one from Winchester and the other from London. These were in constant use by people traveling to Becket's tomb, hoping to be cured of their illnesses and pardoned from their sins.

HENRY VIII AND THE DESTRUCTION OF ENGLISH SHRINES

Partly due to Becket, the church became more and more powerful over the following centuries. Every aspect of life centered on the importance of the Catholic Church and its leader, the pope in Rome. Eventually, some people began to protest against this stranglehold on society. These "protestants" formed their own churches. In England, Henry VIII, who reigned from 1509 to 1547, decided to break away from the pope's authority altogether and become the head of the church in England.

Because of Henry VIII's decision, all the saints' shrines in England were violently broken up. Many shrines, like Saint Thomas's in Canterbury, were elaborately made and covered in precious jewels.

This is a photo of the Trinity Chapel at the east end of Canterbury Cathedral. It was in this part of the cathedral that Becket's shrine was placed. In 1174, four years after his death, Canterbury Cathedral was seriously damaged by fire. The cathedral was rebuilt in a newer style and was greatly enlarged. The huge number of pilgrims visiting Canterbury to see the place of Becket's martyrdom helped pay for this restoration.

Regardless, Henry VIII didn't hesitate. On his orders, Becket's shrine was destroyed. In fact, the destruction was so complete that no one even knew what happened to Becket's bones. In his book *Historical Memorials of Canterbury*, a priest of Canterbury Cathedral, Dean Stanley, noted that on November 16, 1538, Henry VIII issued a royal proclamation commanding that "henceforth [from now on] Thomas Becket shall not be esteemed [honored], named, reputed [given a famous reputation] nor called a Saint . . . and that his images and pictures throughout the whole realm [kingdom] shall be put down and avoided [removed] out of all churches . . ."

That was the end of Becket.

People still visit and pray in Canterbury Cathedral, one of the most beautiful buildings in Britain. Although the shrine is no longer there, the area in the cathedral where Becket was murdered, known today as "the Martyrdom," attracts more than a million visitors every year.

TIMELINE

| 1118 | Thomas Becket is born in London, the son of a prosperous merchant. |

| 1128 | Becket is sent to Merton Priory to be educated by the monks. |

| 1143 | Becket enters the service of the archbishop of Canterbury and begins to go on diplomatic missions on the archbishop's behalf. |

| 1155 | Henry II makes Thomas Becket chancellor, and Becket goes on diplomatic missions on the king's behalf. |

| 1159 | Becket takes part in a military campaign in Toulouse. |

| 1162 | Becket becomes archbishop of Canterbury and resigns as chancellor. |

| 1164 | Becket argues against the king at a meeting held at Clarendon. In the end, he gives in to the king. At another meeting, held at Northampton, Becket defies the king. He flees to France to escape the king's anger. |

| 1170 | On June 14, Henry's son, Henry the Young King, is crowned. Becket is outraged that other bishops have done this in his absence.

In July, Becket and King Henry end their quarrel.

In early December, Becket returns to England and excommunicates those who took part in the coronation of Henry the Young King.

On December 29, four knights murder Becket in Canterbury Cathedral. |

| 1173 | Thomas Becket is declared to be a saint. |

GLOSSARY

abbey   A place where monks or nuns live, work, and pray.

absolution   A pardon granted by a priest to a sinner who is sorry for what he or she has done.

absolve   To pardon a person for his or her sins. Only priests can absolve sinners.

altar   A tablelike block of stone or wood at the far end of a church or chapel. The priest stands at this when celebrating Mass.

archbishop   A senior bishop.

baron   A powerful nobleman and landholder in the Middle Ages.

Canterbury   A city in the southeast corner of England, not far from the coastal town of Dover, which is the seaport nearest to France. Canterbury Cathedral is the place where the most important churchman in England—the archbishop of Canterbury—has his home.

chancellor   The most important officer serving a king during the Middle Ages.

chaplain   The personal priest for important men and women in the Middle Ages. The chaplain said prayers with them and heard their confessions.

consecrated   Blessed by a priest.

Crusades   A series of wars waged by the Christian European leaders during the Middle Ages. The goal was to capture Jerusalem, which was held by the Muslims.

crypt   An underground part of a large church or cathedral. It was often used for private services and personal prayer. Sometimes, people were buried in the cathedral's crypt instead of in the churchyard outside.

deacon   A minor official of the church, lower in rank than a priest.

deed   An act performed by someone—usually an act of great importance.

dictator   A ruler who has unlimited authority in a country, without having a parliament to advise him.

diocese   The area ruled by a bishop, sometimes called a "see." Each bishop has his own diocese. The archbishop of Canterbury has authority over all the dioceses in Britain. Also, he has his own see, in and around Canterbury.

diplomacy   The act of negotiating and making deals, especially with foreign statesmen.

dowry   A gift given at a marriage by the family of the bride to the bridegroom.

dukedom   A province that was ruled by a duke.

dynasty   A family of kings or rulers; a system of government by which each ruler is succeeded by his son or daughter.

Great Council   In the Middle Ages, before any form of parliament had been developed, a king invited the most important noblemen to gather together to hear his commands and perhaps offer advice. This gathering of noblemen was called the Great Council.

hawking   A popular sport in the Middle Ages in which a bird of prey, such as a hawk or a falcon, was specially trained to find and kill other birds. People would carry these birds of prey on their wrists and encourage them to fly off, kill their prey, and then return.

heir   A person who inherits or is expected to inherit something. The heir to the throne is the person who is expected to be king or queen when the old king or queen dies.

House of Commons   In Great Britain, the group of members of Parliament who are elected by the people.

House of Lords   In Great Britain, the group of noblemen who are appointed to help the members of Parliament (MPs) in making laws.

Houses of Parliament   The name given to the combined House of Commons and House of Lords. Both houses are situated in the same building in London, which is called the Palace of Westminster.

interdict   A punishment imposed by the pope on an entire country. Such a punishment was the result of some misdeed committed by the king of that country.

It meant that no church services could be held while the interdict was in force.

jousting   A medieval sport; a mock battle in which two knights on horseback carried long lances or spears with which they tried to knock each other off their horses. It was good training for real warfare, but knights were often injured and even killed in jousting matches.

living   A position held by someone employed by the church. It meant that the person was given a salary.

Magna Carta   A famous document barons forced King John (1199–1216) to sign. John was forced to promise not to imprison people unfairly or to tax them excessively.

martyr   Someone who dies for his or her faith. In the Catholic Church, anyone who dies because of being persecuted is considered to be a martyr.

martyrdom   Dying on the account of one's religious beliefs. In Canterbury Cathedral, the Martyrdom is the name specially given to the place where Thomas Becket was killed.

monk   A man who has undertaken to live a holy life, entirely dedicated to God. He has made a promise to live a life of chastity (that is, never participating in any sexual activity), poverty, and obedience to his superiors.

oath   A solemn declaration (made with a hand on the Bible) to signify that what is said is the undoubted truth.

ordained   Officially blessed and given the rank of a priest.

ordination A church service at which men (and nowa-days women, too) are blessed and become priests.

penitence The state of being sorry and ashamed of one's sins. In the Catholic Church, sinners are expected to confess their wrongdoings to a priest (this is known as confession) and to declare that they are properly sorry. The priest then absolves them, meaning that their sins are forgiven.

reform A change intended to improve an organization.

retinue A company of servants and attendants accompanying a nobleman or king as he travels about the country.

revenues The income received by a church, usually in the form of rent paid by the tenants of the lands owned by that church.

sacrilege The act of destroying or damaging a sacred object or place of worship.

shroud A white sheet (sometimes called a winding-sheet) that is wrapped around a dead body prior to burial.

vassal Someone who is dependent on a superior lord or king and who owes loyalty and obedience to that superior lord.

warden Someone who looks after a building, such as a castle, and is responsible for it.

FOR MORE INFORMATION

WEB SITES
Due to the changing nature of Internet links, the Rosen Publishing Group, Inc., has developed an online list of Web sites related to the subject of this book. This site is updated regularly. Please use this link to access the list:

http://www.rosenlinks.com/lema/tbec

FOR FURTHER READING

Knowles, David. *The Historian and Character*. Cambridge, England: Cambridge University Press, 1955.

Millor, W. J., H. E. Butler, and C. N. L. Brooke. *Letters of John of Salisbury*. London: Nelson Publishers, 1955.

Webb, Diana. *Pilgrimage in Medieval England*. London: Hambledon and London, 2000.

BIBLIOGRAPHY

Barber, Richard. *The Devil's Crown: A History of Henry II and His Sons.* London: The British Broadcasting Corporation, 1978.

Eliot, T. S. *Murder in the Cathedral.* London: Faber and Faber, 1935.

Farmer, David Hugh. *The Oxford Dictionary of Saints.* New York: Oxford, 1987.

Fines, John. *Who's Who in the Middle Ages.* New York: Barnes & Noble, 1970.

Hilliam, David. *Kings, Queens, Bones and Bastards.* Stroud, England: Sutton Publishing, 1998.

Pain, Nesta. *The King and Becket.* London: Eyre & Spottiswoode, 1964.

Weir, Alison. *Eleanor of Aquitaine.* London: Jonathan Cape, 1999.

INDEX

ABOUT THE AUTHOR

David Hilliam grew up in Salisbury and Winchester and was educated at both Oxford and Cambridge Universities. He has taught at schools in Canterbury, London, and Versailles, France. He is passionately interested in the British monarchy. His books include *Kings, Queens, Bones, and Bastards; Monarchs, Murders, and Mistresses;* and his latest, *Crown, Orb, and Sceptre,* which is an account of all the British royal coronations. At present, he lives and works in Dorset, England.

CREDITS

PHOTO CREDITS
Cover (background) pp. 18, 22, 38, 64, 66, 69, 86, 94 © AKG images/British Library; cover (inset), pp. 3, 8, 12 © The Art Archive/Canterbury Cathedral/ Dagli Orti; p. 16 © AKG images/ Visioars; p. 19 © AKG images/Joseph Martin; pp. 30, 80, 91 © Angelo Hornak Photo Library; p. 33 © The National Archives, London; pp. 26–27 © AKG images; pp. 40–41, 77, 96 © AKG images/Erich Lessing; p. 45 © The Art Archive/Dagli Orti; p. 48 © Ken Welsh/The Bridgeman Art Library; p. 50 © Michael Nicholson/Corbis; pp. 58–59, 73 © AKG images/Jean-Paul Dumontier; p. 62 © Skyscan PhotoLibrary/Quick PhotoAir; p. 81 © Bettmann/Corbis; p. 93 © The Art Archive/Musée du Louvre Paris/ Dagli Orti.

Designer: Evelyn Horovicz
Editor: Annie Sommers
Photo Researcher: Elizabeth Loving